Y0-BEM-233

Talking

from

Experience

By Charlene R. Cobbs

PublishAmerica
Baltimore

© 2008 by Charlene R. Cobbs.
All rights reserved. No part of this book may be reproduced, stored in a retrieval system or transmitted in any form or by any means without the prior written permission of the publishers, except by a reviewer who may quote brief passages in a review to be printed in a newspaper, magazine or journal.

First printing

PublishAmerica has allowed this work to remain exactly as the author intended, verbatim, without editorial input.

ISBN: 1-60474-299-2
PUBLISHED BY PUBLISHAMERICA, LLLP
www.publishamerica.com
Baltimore

Printed in the United States of America

Dedications

This book is dedicated to my parents Charlotte and Andy for their undeniable support, to my sisters Andrea and Shay for their effortless dedication, to my nieces and nephew: Chenae, Aiyana, Antonio and Niyah for their consistent flow of inspiration and to my fiancé Saleem for his unconditional love.

Special Acknowledgments

I would like to give special acknowledges to my friends who have inspired and encouraged me through my years of writing. Special thanks also go to Celeste Moore for helping me in my decision to publish this book.

Talking

from

Experience

A Flower

A flower is so beautiful
Life is captured in its stem
Love is inside its petals
In its leaves, courage lies within
So the next time that you see a flower
Pick it up; hold it close to your heart
Because flowers are a lot like people
So easily, they tear apart

Adell

Sometimes he'd beat her so bad
That I could hear her head hitting the wall
Everyone said it was none of my business
I was only the woman across the hall
In my sleep I could hear her screaming
Begging, "please no more"
I'd get up and look through the peephole
And imagine seeing what's happening behind that door
Sometimes I would see her outside the apartment
I wanted to reach out and pull her inside
I figured at least she wouldn't be there when he got home
And in here, I'd help her hide
But I didn't have the courage
I just watched as she went in and closed the door
I wanted to help her
I wanted to do more
But I just sat back and waited
Until it was too late
One day after beating her unconscious
He slit her throat with a piece a broken plate
The police escorted him out
And it seemed like now everyone had a story to tell
Me, I sat crying in my apartment
Regretting not ever doing anything to help Adell

Always

I couldn't ever imagine leaving you behind
You not only captivate the pleasures of my body
You intrigue my mind

Before you there was no one
That could make my heart smile
And the feeling that I feel when you're near me
Had left me stranded for awhile

No one could make my body tingle
Just by licking their lips
No one could make me want them more
Just by grabbing my hips

The feeling I feel when you're around
Is a yearning I can't avoid
The love that you bestow upon me
Is a passion that fills the void

I'll stay with you always
If you promise you will continue to do
Everything that you do to make my life complete
Because I can't imagine life again without you

Before and After

Before you there was no smiling
Just because I wanted to
Before you there was no day-dreaming
There was never any time for me to
Before you there were no holidays
Every day was just another day
Before you there was no sunshine
Every sky was colored with gray
But after you, the smiles disappeared
And the days turned into lonely nights
Each holiday lasted for an eternity
And the sunshine melted out of sight
It seemed like everything that once made me happy
Suddenly made me sad
And everything that I once cherished
Was only what I wished I had

Beyond My Reach

I can see you standing there
But with arms extended, you're just out of my reach
I know that here, there is a lesson to be learned
But if I'm unable to learn it, then who then will I teach
I know in my heart that I can not have you
But that doesn't stop me from wanting you even more
I'm hoping that if you could just hear me knocking
That you would willingly open the door
I guess that if love is naïve
And I still choose to be in it, then so am I
You may be beyond my reach
But I can't give up, I have to at least try

Blind Doubt

Shattered dreams
Bewildered minds
Confused thoughts
All of the time
Cries of doubt
No kind words
"You'll never be nothing"
Was all they heard
So they listened
And with blind doubt
They gave in

Bill of Health

My name is Bill
Woman adore me
Every time I look around,
Someone's checking me out
I can have anyone I want
When and where ever I want them
I'm the man
I had this one girl paying my rent
Another taking care of my car note
One even supplying me with spending money
Who's the PIMP?
Man they just can't get enough of me
And the sex is great!
Morning, noon and night
As a matter of fact,
Just last month, I met this girl named Cheryl
She's so hot that after we finished, I was burning
I mean literally
Yeah, but she's a freak though
So you know, I just hit it and be done with it
Man, relationships are for punks
And so are condoms
There ain't nothing a woman can do for me, but please me
But I'll have to admit, this girl is wearing me out
I've been so tired lately
Even lost some weight
My 215, all muscle, is now 110
I can't even shake a simple cold anymore
That's why I'm here Doc
What's the news?

Dear Aunt Bea

Even years after your passing
These words are hard to say
You were my angel that walked the earth
And it's still hard to accept you've gone away
I think what hurts the most
Is that I didn't get a chance to say goodbye
One of the most important pieces of my life was stolen from me
And my heart still wants to know why
Had I had the chance I would have told you how much I loved you
I would have thanked you for everything you'd done
I would have told you how beautiful I thought you were
That in a contest for the World's Greatest Aunts
You would have been number one
I would have told you that you were like a second mother
The grandmother I never had
A friend when I didn't have anyone to talk to
A counselor when I was feeling sad
You were my Angel
The inspiration that I one day hope to be
God is so lucky to have you
And although He took you too soon, I'm so glad that He shared you
with me

Change

You would think that once life settles in
That things would remain the same
And just when you start to get used to it
Then it goes around and changes
It's like having new and different ideas
Or like making some new friends
It might even be moving to a new location
Or having a new relationship come to an end
It's like needing a new hairstyle
Or wearing a new pair of shoes
In the past these things might not have made a difference
And now you get to choose
You see you can never get too comfortable
Because nothing ever stays the same
Things always become what they were supposed to be
Life is always subject to change

Each and Every One of Us

Each and every one of us
Breathe, eat, sleep and talk
Each and every one of us
Laugh, run, smile and walk
Each and every one of us
Have eyes, a nose and a mouth
We all live in the same world
Be it, East, West, North or South
Each of us cry
Each feels pain
Each have seen the sunshine
Each has felt the rain
Each of us are special
Each black or white
Each of us sleeps under the same sky
During the day or night
Each of us live
Each must die
Each must live together
Each must try

Father Dear

As the Heavens await your arrival
And the angels were sent for your depart
I tried to remember you as you were
And those memories I took to heart
I remembered all that you taught me
And the strength of your iron will
I remembered your overwhelming courage
And thought then, "peace, be still"
I knew that although your body was not with me
You soul would always be one with mine
May you rest in peace eternally
And don't worry about me Father Dear, I'll be just fine

Forever

Forever in my heart
For the rest of my days
Forever in my life
I want you to stay
Forever in my dreams
When I sleep at night
Forever in a daze
When you hold me tight
Forever in my heart
For the rest of my days
Forever I will love you
Don't you ever go away

Have You Ever Noticed How Loud Silence Can Be?

Have you ever noticed how loud silence can be
When words are left waiting to be said
It's like telling someone for the first time that you love them
And you don't get an echo
But a blank stare instead
And then they turn away and day dream
And you're left to assume the worst
Wishing that you could take back what you just said
And had let them say it first

I Found Happiness

I've searched the world for happiness
And in each empty space was you
I've searched every inch of my heart for love
And guess what, you were there too
I thought about all the lonely times
When I really needed a friend
And just when I thought that no one cared
You saw an opportunity and you rushed in
I've searched oh so long for someone to make me complete
And just when it seemed that my search was through
I found that sought after happiness
Right here, with you

I Love You

I love you spiritually
With my mind, body and soul
I love you agelessly
What I feel for you can never grow old
I love you differently
Than anyone who has ever loved you before
I love you unknowingly
No woman could love you more

I Promise

I promise to love you faithfully
If you promise to love me
I promise to always be there
If you promise you will be
I promise to give you all my love
My mind, body and soul
I promise to try to keep you safe
Together we can grow old
I promise to miss you when you leave
And to blossom when you return
If you promise to do the same for me
Whenever it's my turn
I promise to do all for you
That I could possibly do
Not because I would want something in return
Just because, I love you

I Release You, I Too Am Finally Free

Roses are red
Violets are blue
The games that you played
Backfired on you
You took my heart
And threw it to the ground
Destroyed my pride
You let me down
But no more
We've grown apart
I've let you go
I deserve a new start
And the snake you've become
Is what you will always be
But your wicked ways
No longer include me
So goodbye to you
You are finally free
My shackles no longer hold you
Where you do not wish to be

I Waited for You

I knocked gently on your front door
And it opened just enough for me to get inside
I stepped in and looked around for minute
And then the kid in me wanted to get behind the door and hide
So that when you walked through it
I could jump out and yell surprise
The thought of the amazement on your face made me laugh
I imagined the funny look you would have in your eye
So I decided to just leave a note instead
That said…while you were gone…I waited for you….
Call me when there's better time for me to come see you again
And then I'll come back through

I Remember

I remember when I was just a child
I used to dream of far away lands
I remember when I was a teenager
Back then I had so many plans
And now that I'm an adult
Things seem so much easier back than
Now the more I seem to lose
The harder it is to win
I remember when I was getting ready for college
I was afraid but ready to explore
Then once I got a taste for knowledge
I wanted even more and more
And my good times became monuments
I had never had so much fun
Then one day I graduated
And the first day of my life begun
And now I look back and wonder
My, where does the time fly
My heart recaptures all the memories
And tears drop down from my eyes
But I've got to keep on going
There's a world out there, just waiting for me
I have people I haven't even met yet
And places I'd one day like to be
I'm a grown up now
And may Lord have mercy on me
My past I pray I'll never forget
Or how life was so sweet to me

I'd Give to You

To you I give my heart
That's wider than the Arabian Sea
To you I give my soul
The sweetest essence of me
To you I give my faith
The only thing that keeps me strong
To you I give my courage
To help you carry on
To you I give my love
So that you can feel what it is that I feel
To you I give my honesty
So that you can know what I feel is real
I'd give you a world of diamonds
Memories that last longer than gold
In return I ask for your priceless love
To cherish as we grow old

Animal Magnetism

I smile as I watch you sleeping
My fingers can't help but ran along your skin
The warmness between my legs wants to awaken you
So that it can welcome you back in
Instead I just lay close beside you
Your body moves to intertwine with mine
Soft kisses I plant on the nape of your neck
As I reach my hand around you to find
The place that had softened in slumber
Has awaken and is a full grown beast
Like a lioness I'm hungry for adventure
And patiently await my feast......

If I Were a Butterfly

If I were a butterfly
I'd fly as high as the eye can see
I wouldn't worry about flying too low
Because no one's net could ever capture me
If I were a butterfly
I'd be as different as I could be
I'd be joyful and full of color
Like a peacock or a bumble bee
I'd smile at the ooo's and ahh's
Hold my chest out to the compliments
Why I'd even do a few tricks
Put on a show of entertainment
If I were a butterfly
No more constraints, I'd finally be free
And I'd leave this old world behind
Letting my spirit soar within the breeze

I'm Special Now

I used to feel neglected
Like if I died no one would even care
I used to limit my conversation
Because when I would speak, my words no one would hear
I used to be controlled by everyone
I didn't know my left from my right
Criticism was a simple as someone saying hello
I wasn't acknowledged simply by sight
But here I am, standing proud and tall
And I dare you not to look at me
You will respect the woman that I have become
Don't waste your time on jealousy and envy
I'm doing things with my life I never dreamed I could do
Enjoying my life and no one has to tell me how
Leaving behind the no body I used to be
Look at me I'm special now

Last Night

Last night
Fingers gently slide up and down my back
I didn't open my eyes
I laid there and smiled
As my body warmed to the touch
Every time they'd cross over the middle of my back
My body would jerked, it felt comfortable
Last night
I felt a body laying behind mine
I felt him breathing on my neck
Then tender kisses on my shoulders
I turned to face my accuser with curiosity
Who was this theft of passion laying behind me
It was you
Last night
I kissed you
Touched you
Tasted you
Made love to you
In every position imaginable
Last night
I thought of you
Those thoughts lingers in my mind still today

Let Me Speak to Your Heart

Here me heart
Let not your ears be covered by ignorance of the unknown
I have loved you from first I saw you
But know that that which separates us, is a wall of unbearable bounds
And it not my destiny to climb it
So sadly I except loves failure with pride
And go on with my life
But never to forget what once was
And what will always be
The heart whose words will be spoken
Will always speak to thee

My Little Blessings

First there was Chenae
An inquisitive little girl
She went from Barney and Mickey Mouse
to boys, cars and pin curls
Then there was Aiyana
The Gerber baby that was tough as nails
She went through the Teletubbie era
to getting pedicures and painted toe nails
And along came little Antonio
the sweetie pie who wanted to be everyone's friend
Now, the video game king
whose walk-in closet he remodeled into a den
And last but not least we have Niyah
Our busy baby bumble bee
Her energy that's almost unbearable
But you can just call her Ms. Personality
No matter how different they may be
There's one thing that they all share
They are all Aunt Charlene's little blessings
No matter how old they get, the love I have for them, will always be there

Love 'Em and Leave 'Em

Love 'em and leave 'em
How soon we forget
It's easy to play games
But it's hard to bare regret
The men think they can get any woman
And the woman think they can always find another man
Those grown people should be ashamed of themselves
A thing called a conscious should be in demand
Love, at one time, used to be sacred
Now cheating has become our biggest fan
Because wedding vows now symbolize nothing more
than a piece of paper and a golden band

Mr. Perfect?

About five foot nine
Maybe six two
The blacker the berry
The sweeter the juice
A nice set of teeth
Oh yeah and some dimples will do
A nicely built body
Lord make him bowlegged too
Now let's not forget about his personality
A sense of humor would be nice
He's got to be charming and adventurous
A romantic to entice
And if he can't be perfect
How about two out of three?
And Lord when you finish with him
You can finish your work on me

My Last Words

If I could give you anything worth giving
I'd give you my heart
If I were to write a movie of my life
You'd be written into one of the best part
If I were to write a novel,
I'd call it "Me and You"
If I could do anything right now
It would be whatever you wanted to do
I've never really been good at good-byes
So, instead of goodbye, I'll see you the next time
And to be honest, I don't have any last words for you
Because every time I write, I'm speaking to you in every line

My Soulmate

You're everything that I've ever dreamed of
All that I thought you would be
God was flawless in His creation of you
Not perfect but perfect for me
I smile at the mere thought of you
I blush just thinking about being in your arms
Captivated I am by every word that you speak
Taken away by your dazzling charm
Who else could you be, but my soulmate?
Who else would you be able to so easily mend my heart?
Who else could you be, but my soulmate?
Who came from out of no where, holding every missing part
You restored my body with life
It was you who gave me back my dignity
If ever I were to find out that you were not my soulmate
It wouldn't matter; I'd still want you here with me

Never

I never got any roses
Never been serenaded under a tree
No late night strolls on the beach
No one ever proposed to me
Never got any sky-written messages of love
Or had a romantic picnic in the park
Never had a song named after me
Or had my name carved out in tree bark
Never celebrated an anniversary
Never even got a friendship ring
Never had anyone gaze deep into my eyes
Never once felt my heart sing
Never been told, "I love you"
In a reassuring voice
But always had a broken heart
With or without a choice

No Sweeter Love

I love like no other before or after me
Therefore, for you my love is unique
I can give you whatever it is that you need
And provide you still with whatever it is that you seek
Call me a fool or learn from me
Realize that with me you can't go wrong
I will be to you that sweet musical melody
In that so wanted to hear love song
There won't be a day that goes by without smiling
Or a night that is not filled with moans
A week that doesn't bring us even closer
Or a year that our love hasn't grown
And if ever there shall be a love that goes down in history
It will be ours that all will treasure
It will be a day that God has made
It will be yours and mine forever

Picture of Life

Picture ecstasy
Painted by you and I
Picture harmony
You by my side
Picture confusion
Who is she to intrude?
Picture anger
Words that we shared were rude
Picture sorrow
That of which I paint alone
Picture a broken heart
There's no longer a happy home
Picture a teardrop
They fall in a single line
Picture me
Once again left behind

Picture on the Wall

There's something in that picture
For pictures do not stare
For every where I walk
Its eyes are starring there
I tried to catch it one time
But it was just too smart
I think I'll use a hammer
Or throw at it a dart
I'm tired of being watched
By the picture on the wall
I think I'll go and move it
With the pictures in the hall

Prayers Bring Close Impossible Loves

I've fallen for a gentleman
Tall as an ebony tree
Who knows not that he makes my heart sing
And buzz like a dancing bee
He makes my smile run like the river
And my souls fly like a bird who knows she's free
If prayers bring close impossible loves
Then please bring my gentleman to me

Simply Does

Sometimes we look for things
Because we want them to be there
We fall in love with the wrong people
Because we want someone to care
Sometimes we hurt people
For no apparent reason at all
And some of us who are fortunate
Want to see the unfortunate ones falls
But who will help somebody
With no reward in return
And who will mend the boards
Of the bridges already burnt
And who is simply happy
Just because
I am and who ever feels exactly the way I do
Simply does

Reconstruction

What can I say?
When all is said and done
What can I do?
When the battle I've lost is won
What can I have?
When what was here is now gone
I have but no choice left
But to carry on
The hill of "black pride" slowly slopes
Causing us to slip and fall
We've weathered every one of the storms
And we've given it our all
But when all the weapons repeal
What are we left with to fight?
Should we just sleep all day?
While they sit up and think all night
No, we should work on reconstruction
Building back up our house
Fear should not overcome us
For we are man not mouse
When we sang, "we shall overcome"
The words shall read, "we already overcame"
Stand out, black children
And be proud of your name

Second to No One

You were not free when I met you
Though I was under the impression that things would soon change
So, I trusted you with my love and friendship
Yet even with time, that was all that remained
First it was you sneaking off at night to meet me
Now you're delegating how I spend my time
You're wondering whose that man calling my house
Have you forgotten that you're her man, not mine?
Now you want me to express my feelings for you
To leave my heart open wide
So you could know just what strings to pull
While your own feelings you choose to hide
Look, I know it was wrong to mess with you in the first place
And to correct that, I've choose mind over demeanor
Yes, one day I will reap what I have sown
But without you, the grass looks oh so much greener

Someone I Used to Know

I saw him standing on the corner of Fifth and Lexington
Waiting for the light to change before walking across the street
His face seemed so familiar
And I knew at one time, we had had a chance to meet
I wanted to get a closer look
So I followed him into a café
And sure enough he was who I thought he was
But he was aged a bit by a life of dismay
I watched him from a distance
Saddened by his unhappy sigh
He appeared not to have a lot of money
And only ordered a slice of Lemon Meringue Pie
I finally wandered over
And my words whispered as so,
"Hello my dear father",
"Am I somebody you used to know?"

Farewell

I know that you had no idea of my leaving you so soon
But life's expectations can take us all by surprise
Don't think of my leaving as a departure
But as a horizon of a new sunrise
I'll miss all of you very much
From the smiles down to the frowns
And even though I'm moving to a new place
In your hearts, I'll always be around

Saleem

Long thick locks
Covering his bedroom eyes
Soft full lips
When he speaks his words memorize
Big strong arms
That hold me like a steal cage
A hard chocolate chest
Laying against it calms my rage
He rocks me like a cradle
And never has to say a word
His silence is so relaxing
Everything he didn't say, I heard
When he does speak he says, " I love you"
And I say, "I love you too"
Then I close my eyes and go to a place that resembles Heaven
And he whispers, "Let me go with you"

Charlotte and Andy

I could say that I have the best parents in the world
And it would be a true statement to me
Everything that I am in this life
My parents brought that to be
My professionalism I get from my mother
But my supervisory style I get from my dad
Mom taught me to be serious and firm with my employees
But dad said mingle and laugh
My personality is a mixture of the two
Dad's the reason I crack jokes and love to cut the fool
Mom's well balanced and educated
She's the reason I'm a scholar in school
As a hobby I love to fix things
That definitely came from dad
Mom's a jazzy dresser
She keeps me from wearing strips with plaid
Dad likes technology so I'm a computer geek
Mom likes everything clean and neat
With my busy schedule, I'm still perfecting that technique
Both of my parents are compassionate
Which inspires my writing style
Mom likes to go home early
But dad could stay awhile
Both like to take road trips
The reason I love to travel
Mom is a strong debater
Dad just laughs at the sound of the gavel
And as different as they may be
When making me, they definitely agree
I am my father or maybe my mothers child
One of the three creations of Charlotte and Andy

The Sun

He smiled at me
And his rays of love warmed my day
As I traveled
I noticed he was following me
But not a word did he say
Our shadows began to work hand in hand
And soon he was laid to sleep
His brother now watched over the earth
While I too, slumbered deep

Teardrops

Slowly burning an endless trail
Tracking the structure of my cheek
Teardrops fall one by one
Draining me until I become weak
The taste of salt and water
I taste it on my tongue
I started out with a sea
Now a river has begun
I can't stop these teardrops from falling
Into an endless well
Teardrops they just keep on falling
My eyes are beginning to swell

Touch Me

Smooth buttery skin
Light brown caramel eyes
Full rose colored lips
A smile used to mesmerize
Touch me and light my insides on fire
Touch me and make my juices flow
Touch me, whenever you need to
Touch me, you won't hear me say no
Touch me, let me feel your hands on my body
Touch me, don't be afraid to pull and bite
Touch me anywhere you want to
Make me call our your name tonight
Touch me, until I reach my full climax
Then hold me until I fall asleep
Rub my back as I lay close beside you
And together we can slumber deep

Understand This

How can I begin to understand you,
When you obviously don't understand me
Black is my skin color
Not a reason for you to dislike me
I can't change who I am
No would I, if I could
I will never bow to evil
I stand tall and strong like wood
Because I am the truth
And the truth bares the light
You can try to overlook me
But God corrects all sight
Understand this

Virgin

It's ok to be different
But only few think so
You don't have to say yes
If you really mean no
Your virginity should be taken lightly
It's a sacred part of who you are
You should cherish it like precious diamonds
Not wear it like an unwanted scar
Waiting is only asking a little
But spreading too much of yourself is giving a lot
We should all be our own person
Instead of being someone that we are not
And if you think being a virgin isn't cool
Then you've got a lot to learn
Virginity is something you don't have to work for
But once you have sex, you pay for the consequences that you earn

Wasn't So Long Ago

Wasn't so long ago
When we were each other's friend
Seems like just yesterday
Our love came to an end
Wasn't so long ago
That we consumed each other's space
Now you're just a memory
A name without a face
Wasn't so long ago
When you loved me as I still love you
How soon we forget
The ones we once belonged to

Why Do People Cry?

I wonder what makes people cry
For tears to come out of their eyes
The feeling is just depressing
To see someone that needs your caressing
I wonder what makes people cry
I really don't mean to pry
I just thought it polite if I
Ask why those tears fall from your eyes

Will I Love You Tomorrow?

Will I love you tomorrow?
Do you even have to ask?
Loving you any day of the week
To me, is the easiest task
To give you even the smallest part of me
Is to have given you a treasure to keep
My love flows as long as the Nile River
And my soul travels just as deep
Every moment is a moment of pleasure
As I will satisfy your every desire you have within
Will I love you tomorrow is not the question
The question is will the love I have for you ever end

Sisters

If you don't have any, you won't understand
how special they are
its not always about being able to wear their clothes
or being able to fit their shoes
it's much more than that
it's like having a special friend that's always there
that knows what you're going through personally
spiritually, emotionally
it's being able to talk to them about anything
and you can laugh or cry or even argue or fight
but still love them in the end because of their honesty
and they will always tell the truth, even if it hurts
whether you want to hear it or not
and even through all your pain from hearing the truth
you can still appreciate it and take it to heart
because you know they are the protectors that keep you safe
they are sometimes second mothers
the doctors when your injured
healers of broken hearts
they're counselors
their friends
and most of all they are family
they are my sisters and I love them dearly

Who Am I Fooling?

How could a guy like him?
Ever want a girl like me
I mean he's so handsome and talented
And me, well I'm just me
He's so sophisticated, hardworking and successful
And I'm ordinary, caring and sincere
Let's not forget with a good sense of humor
And when I'm needed, I'm always there
But how much weight could those qualities carry
I'm no model by any means
What athlete you know marries your average woman?
It's been a long time since I saw a real sistah on the benches routing for her team
I haven't got a chance
Even though I'm educated, I cook and take good care of myself
I'm talented, good with computes and can fix almost anything
I've assembled entertainment systems, computer desks and book shelves
I write poetry, I sing, and have even played the flute once
I'm a people person, help in the community, I've even helped plant trees
I might not be a model, but I'm more gracious
I too have style, grace and when it comes to my man, I know how to please
Come to think of it I'm a wonderful person
Any man should be proud to have one of these
But who am I fooling; Tony Gonzales is so beyond my reach
And I might not be able to touch him, but he's all mine in my dreams

Talking from Experience

These words are mine
With them, you don't have to agree
They came from my life and from past experiences
Of those that are or were close to me
I gladly share them with you
And you can take them where ever you please
If only a paragraph of my words, could affect just one life
Then this troubled old heart will be at ease
I'm just talking from experience
You don't have to travel the road that I have
I'm just talking from experience
This is my baggage so you get your own bags
Everybody has to live their own lives
We all have to go through things
Words just make it a little easier to tell the stories
Sometimes they bring happiness through all the pain
So when you may be going through
And you just need some encouraging thoughts
Flip the pages of my experiences
I hope you find the peace that's sought

Printed in the United States
105033LV00003B/190-198/A

9 781604 742992